NICOLA KINNEAR

Can I PLAY?

ALISON GREEN BOOKS

George had his very own island,
all to himself. It was just perfect.
"With your own island," thought George,
"you can do whatever you like."

And George liked doing
all sorts of things.

He wondered sometimes about having a friend, but friends were tricky.

What if they wanted to play something different?

What if they ruined his games?

Or even laughed at him? That would be terrible.

Then one day, George was howling a song,

Ow-ow-ooOOOO!!!

when he heard a funny noise – a sort of echo:

ow-ow-oooOOO!

And when he was practising his cartwheels,
he heard an odd clapping sound:

Flip-Flap-FLAP!

That was strange.
It could only mean one thing.

There was someone else on his island!
George was horrified.

He hid behind a rock.
But whatever it was came closer and closer.
Then he heard a sneeze, and a shuffle . . .

. . . and a little seal wiggled up to him.

"Can I play?" asked the seal.

"My name's Pebble. We could be friends!"

"I don't like friends," said George.

"Friends just ruin things."

"I don't!" said Pebble.

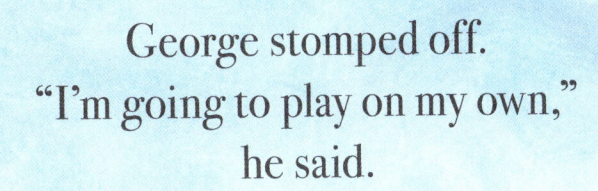

George stomped off.
"I'm going to play on my own,"
he said.

"Good idea," said Pebble. "I'll come, too,"
and she wriggled after him.

After that, whatever George played,
Pebble played, too. George tried ignoring
her, but she was really annoying.

She got in the way of all his photos,

she ruined his drawing,

she was far too good at
roly-polying

and she liked really
stinky snacks.

George had had enough.
"I'm going to do some dancing,"
he said, glumly. "On my own."
"Good idea," said Pebble.
"I'll come, too."

But as soon as George started dancing,
Pebble rolled about laughing.
"You look really funny!" she said.

"No, I don't," said George, but Pebble kept on giggling.

George stopped dancing and glared at her.
"Oh, don't stop!" said Pebble.
"I like your dancing."

"You just like making fun of me," growled George, and he stormed off.

He set off up the highest hill on the island.
"Wait!" cried Pebble. "I can't climb up there!"
"Good!" said George.

"I didn't mean to upset you," called Pebble.
"Look! I've found you a lucky shell."

"I don't want your lucky shell!"
shouted George. "I want you to go away!"

Pebble watched him sadly
for a moment, then she waddled
into the sea, to play on her own.

George sulked for a while. But then he started
to wonder if he'd been a bit mean.

It felt very quiet, without Pebble around.
He even felt a little bit lonely.

He was about to go and look for her, when
he heard a squeak, far out to sea.

George peered through his binoculars.
It was Pebble! Was she in trouble?

George scampered down the jetty.
He could see Pebble, surrounded by dolphins.
They'd taken her bobble hat, and wouldn't give it back.

No matter how hard she tried, the dolphins could
always jump higher, just out of her reach.
George gasped. "That's so mean!"

He was very angry. He jumped into his boat, and sailed
towards them as fast as he could. Then he shouted . . .

The dolphins were so surprised,
they dropped Pebble's hat, and splashed
away under the waves.

Pebble beamed at him, wide-eyed.
"Did you say *friend?*" she gasped.

George looked a bit embarrassed.
"I suppose I did," he said. "But I'm
still going to play on my own."

"Good idea," said Pebble. "I'll come, too."

George and Pebble played
all sorts of games.

They did things slightly
differently,

but that didn't seem to
matter any more.

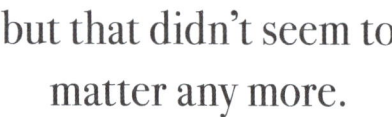

Then George showed off his dancing,
and Pebble joined in, too.

"That was fun," said George.
"I think I'll play on my own again tomorrow."
"I'll come, too," said Pebble.

"Good idea," said George.
"I'd like that."

First published in the UK in 2022 by
Alison Green Books
An imprint of Scholastic
1 London Bridge, London SE1 9BA
Scholastic Ireland, 89E Lagan Road,
Dublin Industrial Estate,
Glasnevin, Dublin D11 HP5F
www.scholastic.co.uk
Designed by Zoë Tucker

HB ISBN: 978 1 407199 64 1
PB ISBN: 978 1 407199 65 8

Paper made from wood grown in responsible
and other controlled forest resources.

1 3 5 7 9 10 8 6 4 2